KB157307

AIRLINE SERVICE ENGLISH

항공 서비스 영어

Preface

항공 객실 서비스는 전문적인 업무 이해도와 다양한 상황에 대처할 수 있는 실무능력뿐만 아니라 세계 여러 나라 고객들에게 최상의 서비스를 제공하기 위해 국제적인 커뮤니케이션 능력이 필수 역량으로 요구되고 있습니다.

그리하여 본 교재는 항공 서비스 학과 재학생 및 국내 외국 항공사 취업을 준비하는 예비승무원들에게 항공 객실 서비스 업무의 이해도 및 항공 영어에 대한 이해를 바탕으로 항공 실무에 대한 전문적인 지식을 습득함과 동시에 이를 영어로 학습하여 실무적인 역량과 국제적 커뮤니케이션 능력을 함양할 수 있도록 합니다. 더 나아가 항공사 근무 중인 현직 객실 승무원들에게는 현장에서 적용할 수 있는 다양한 서비스 및 안전 관련 상황에 대한 영어 단어 및 표현을 통해 국제적 업무역량 향상에 도움이 될 수 있도록 하였습니다.

본 교재는 NCS(National Competency Standard, 국가직무능력표준)를 기반으로 재구성하였으며, 총 크게 Unit4로 구성되어 있으며, Unit 1은 탑승부터 이륙 전 안전 업무에 관한 세부 내용이며 Unit 2는 이륙 후 전반적인 기내 서비스에 관련된 업무, Unit 3은 착륙 준비부터 승객 하기 후 업무, Unit 4는 기내 안에서 빈번히 발생하는 안전 및 서비스 관련 상황들을 다루고 있습니다.

챕터별로 객실 서비스 업무의 이해를 돕기 위한 업무별 이론을 한국어로 설명하였으며, 업무별 이해를 바탕으로 본격적인 영어 표현들을 학습하기 전 업무 관련 영어 어휘를 학습한 뒤 실무영어 표현들과 상황별 다이얼로그로 구성되어 있어 단계별로 쉽고 흥미롭게 학습할 수 있도록 하였습니다. 각 장은 Vocabulary - Practical Expression - Dialogue - Group Activity- Fill in the blank- Match- Translate between Korean and English- Role-play로 구성되어 있습니다.

본 교재를 통하여 항공사 취업을 희망하는 미래의 예비승무원에게는 글로벌 서비스 무대 데뷔를 위한 좋은 자료로 활용될 수 있기를 희망합니다. 끝으로 이 책이 완성되기까지 함께 힘써주셨던 많은 동료 교수님들과 교재를 출간하기 위해 많은 노력을 해주신 한올 출판사 모든 직원분께 감사의 뜻을 전합니다.

Contents

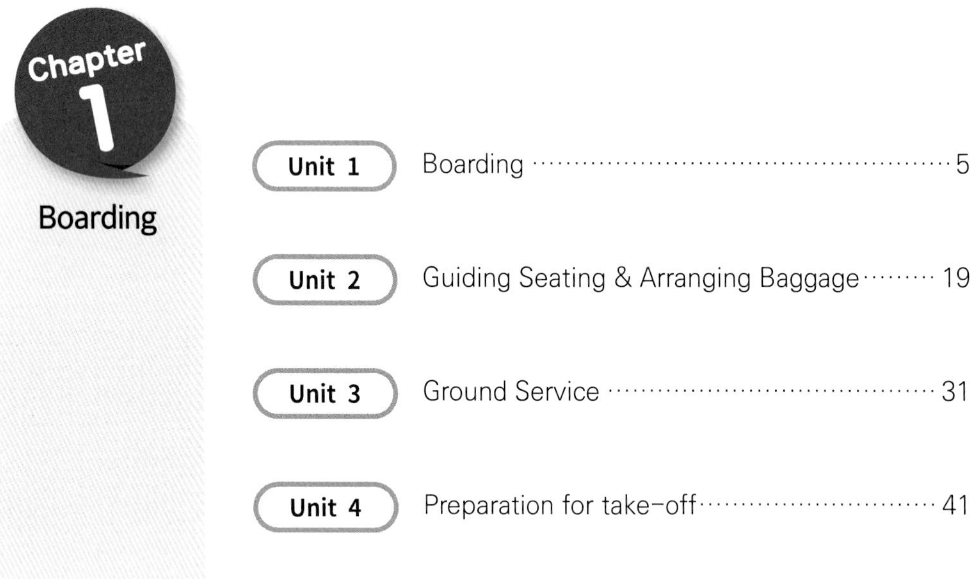

Preparation for landing

Safety and service issue

Chapter 1

Boarding

탑승

Airline Services English

직무설명

객실승무원 탑승 업무의 종류

Preparation for boarding(Pre- flight check Boarding)

기내안전 및 보안점검 업무

- 객실승무원은 항공기 탑승 후 안전보안 및 서비스 설비와 기물을 점검한다.

기내서비스 물품 및 설비 점검

- 객실승무원은 승객 탑승 전 객실 서비스용품의 점검,객실 서비스용품의 배열,서비스 설비 점검 ,입국서류 점검 ,면세품 점검 및 특별 서비스 요청 사항들을 점검한다.

Passenger Boarding

- 승객 탑승은 비행 출발 약 30분 전에 실시되는데, 승무원은 각자 정해진 구역에 위치에서 탑승하는 승객에게 환영 인사를 하기 위해 대기한다. 그리고 승객 탑승 시 탑승권을 확인한다. 객실안에 객실승무원은 승객의 좌석 안내를 도와준다.

Unit 1

Boarding
탑승

Vocabulary of Boarding

No.	English	Korean
1	facility	시설
2	equipment	장비
3	flight information	비행정보
4	galley	갤리(기내주방)
5	oven, coffer maker	오븐, 커피메이커
6	cart(bar cart, meal cart)	카트(바 카트,식사카트)
7	AVOD(Audio & Video on Demand)	주문형 오디오 및 비디오 (기내 엔터테인먼트 시스템 서비스)
8	duty-free Items	면세품
9	Special Service Request(SSR)	특별서비스 요청
10	special service item	특별서비스 물품
11	Unaccompanied Minor(UM)	비 동반 소아
12	F/C: First Class B/C: Business Class E/Y(Economy Class) = Y/C(Economy Class)	퍼스트 클래스 비즈니스클래스 이코노미 클래스
13	boarding pass	탑승권
14	special Meal	특별식

* 각 항공사마다 서비스용어 상이할 수 있음

Practical Expression

1. Welcoming and greeting the customers

Good morning, afternoon, evening.

Welcome **aboard**.

Welcome **on board**.

It's **great** / **good** / **wonderful** to have you aboard.

2. Checking Boarding pass

May I see your boarding pass, please?

Could I see your boarding pass, please?

3. Checking Boarding pass

Please use this aisle.

go down that aisle.

proceed to the other aisle.

Your seat is in the front of the cabin on the left.

middle on the right.

back

It's an aisle seat.

a window

DIALOGUE

Checking the number of passengers and service items prior to passenger boarding

Cabin Service Director

Cabin Crew1

SITUATION 1 Checking Boarding pass

There are 3 first-class passengers, 13 business-class passengers, and 220 economy-class passengers on this flight.

In economy class, we have 10 special meal requests.

Please check all service items and equipment properly.

In first class, everything is perfect.

In business class, the 2 special meals have not been loaded.

In economy class, we don't have headsets.

Okay. I've informed the catering service staff of these issues.

If you find any other problems, please let me know.

SITUATION 2 Checking Boarding pass

C: Good morning, sir. Welcome on board.
Could I see your boarding pass, please?

P: Okay, here it is.

C: Thank you, sir.
Your seat number is 56A. Please take the aisle to your right.

P: Thanks.

C: My pleasure. Have a nice flight.

SITUATION 3 Checking Boarding pass

Good evening, sir. Welcome on board.
May I see your boarding pass, please?

It's in my pocket and I have already checked where my seat is.

We must check each passenger's boarding passes for security reasons, which includes checking your seat number.

Okay. Here it is.

Thank you for your cooperation. Your seat is in the back of the cabin on your left.

Thank you.

It's my pleasure. Have a nice flight.

SITUATION 4 Checking Boarding pass

Good evening, sir. Welcome on board.
May I see your boarding pass, please?

It's in my pocket and I have already checked where my seat is.

We must check each passenger's boarding passes for security reasons, which includes checking your seat number.

Okay. Here it is.

Thank you for your cooperation.
Your seat is in the back of the cabin on your left.

Thank you.

SITUATION 5 Assisting the customers during passenger boarding

Good afternoon, ma'am. It's great to have you on board.

My seat number is 31A. Where is my seat?

Your seat is in the back of the cabin on your right side.
It's a window seat.

Thank you.

Take turns practicing role-playing with your partners.

Situation 1. Pre-flight boarding

Situation 2. Passenger boarding

FILL IN THE BLANK

1. Good morning, Welcome ______________ .

2. It's ______________ to have you aboard.

3. ______________ see your boarding pass, please?

MATCH

A. My boarding pass is in my pocket, and I have already checked where my seat is. •

B. Where is my seat? •

C. Please check all service items and equipment properly. •

• 1. Your seat is in the back of the cabin on your right side.

• 2. We must check each passenger's boarding passes for security reasons, which includes checking your seat number.

• 3. Everything is okay in first class.

TRANSLATE BETWEEN KOREAN AND ENGLISH

1. 다음 문장을 영어로 바꾸어 보세요.

❶ 좋은 오후입니다. 탑승을 환영합니다.

______________________________.

❷ 천만예요, 좋은 비행 되십시오.

______________________________.

❸ 탑승권을 볼 수 있을까요?

______________________________.

2. 다음 문장을 한국어로 바꾸어 보세요

❶ There are 3 first-class passengers, 13 business-class passengers, and 220 economy-class passengers on this flight. In economy class, we have ten special meal requests.

______________________________.

❷ In business class, 2 special meals have not been loaded.

______________________________.

❸ Please check all service items and equipment properly.

____

Situation

What would you say as a cabin crew if a passenger refused to show his boarding pass during passenger boarding?

Your Action

____.

____.

____.

INTERVIEW QUESTIONS

Question 1

What are the responsibilities of a cabin crew before passenger boarding?

Answer 1

____.

____.

항공 서비스 영어

직무설명

좌석 안내 및 수하물 정리

좌석 안내 업무

객실 승무원은 객실내에 승객의 좌석배정에 이상이 없는지 확인하고, 객실 서비스 규정에 따라 좌석 배열을 파악하고 승객을 정확한 좌석으로 안내할 수 있도록 한다.

비상구 열 좌석에는 비상 상황이 발생했을 때 비상 탈출을 도와줄 수 있는 승객에게 좌석을 배정하는데 협조자로서 적합한 승객의 탑승 여부를 확인하고 해당 승객에게는 비상시에 대비하여 비상구 좌석 착석에 관련한 브리핑을 실시한다. 그리고 항공기도어를 닫기 전에 캐빈매니저에게 이상 유무를 보고한다. 또한, 승무원의 좌석 안내가 속히 이루어지지 않으면 항공기 출발에도 지장을 줄 수 있다. 따라서 승무원에 의한 좌석안내는 신속, 정확해야 한다.

수하물 정리 및 지원 업무

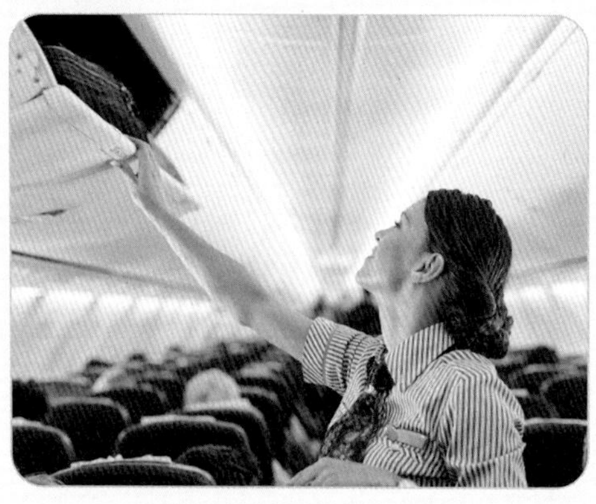

객실승무원은 규정에 따라 수하물을 특성별로 보관가능한 장소에 보관하도록 안내하고, 수하물을 안전하게 다룰 수 있도록 한다.

Unit 2

Guiding Seating & Arranging Baggage

좌석 안내 및 수하물 정리

Vocabulary of In-flight Service

No.	English	Korean
1	overhead bin	(기내) 선반
2	carry-on baggage	(항공기 기내까지 가지고 탈 수 있는) 휴대 가능 수하물
3	seating arrangement	좌석배정
4	emergency exit row	비상구열(좌석)
5	ABP(Able-Bodied Passenger)	(비상탈출을 도와줄수 있는) 몸이 건강한 승객
6	store	보관하다
7	put	(특정한 장소·위치에) 놓다
8	stow	(안전한 곳에) 넣다
9	coat room	코트룸
10	aisle seat / window seat	통로 좌석/창가 좌석

* 각 항공사마다 서비스용어 상이할 수 있음

Practical Expression

1. when cabin crew guides seating during passenger boarding

Certainly, Absolutely, Definitely
Allow me to show you to your seat.
Have a wonderful flight.
May I assist you to your seat?

2. Situation about sitting in the wrong seat

I am sorry for your inconvenience.
Let me check it. Would you mind waiting for a while?
Thank for waiting.

3. Arranging the baggage

I am sorry for your inconvenience.
Let me organize your bags in the overhead bin.
Here is some space for you.
You can store your bags in the overhead bin or under the seat in front of you.

DIALOGUE

SITUATION 1 Assisting seating during passenger boarding

C: Good evening, ma'am. Welcome aboard.

P: My seat number is 11A. I don't know where my seat is. Could you help me?

C: Absolutely, ma'am. Allow me to show you to your seat.

P: Thanks.

C: My pleasure. This is your seat.

P: Thank you so much.

C: You're welcome. Have a wonderful flight.

DIALOGUE

Cabin Crew

passenger 1

passenger 2

SITUATION 2 Situation about sitting in the wrong seat

P1: Excuse me, there is the problem about my seat. Please help me.

C: Definitely, sir.

P1: That seat is supposed to be my seat. However, it is already occupied.

C: I am sorry for your inconvenience. Let me check it. Would you mind waiting for a while?

P1: Okay.

(*Cabin crew approach to Passenger 2*)

C: Excuse me, sir. May I see your boarding pass to check your seat number?

P2: Okay. This is my boarding pass.

Thank you. I am sorry but I am afraid that your seat is behind this seat.

Really? I am sorry.

No problem. Have a great flight.

(*Cabin crew explains the situation and guides the seat to Passenger 1*)

Thank for waiting. Have a nice flight.

Thanks a lot.

SITUATION 3 Arranging the baggage: big suitcase under the seat

Excuse me, ma'am. This suitcase is too big to store under the seat.
Please put this suitcase in the overhead bin.

Oh, I will

Thank you for your cooperation.

SITUATION 4 Arranging the baggage

Excuse me, I can't find any spaces around me to store my bag.

I am sorry for your inconvenience, let me organize your bags in the overhead bin. Here is some space for you. You can stow your bag here.

Thank you so much.

Take turns practicing role-playing with your partners.

Situation 1. Assisting seating

Situation 2. Arranging the baggage

FILL IN THE BLANK based on Dialogue.

1. ______________ I assist you to your seat?

2. Would you mind putting your bag in ______________.

3. ______________ know if you need assistance in stowing your baggage?

MATCH

A. I don't know where my seat is. Could you help me? •

B. That seat is supposed to be my seat. •

C. Excuse me, I can't find any spaces around me to store my bag •

• 1. I am sorry for your inconvenience. Let me check it. Would you mind waiting for a while?

• 2. Absolutely, ma'am. Allow me to show you to your seat

• 3. I am sorry for your inconvenience, let me organize your bags in the overhead bin.

TRANSLATE BETWEEN KOREAN AND ENGLISH

1. 다음 문장을 영어로 바꾸어 보세요.

① 실례하겠습니다, 이 수트 케이스는 너무 커서 좌석 밑에 보관하시기에 너무 큽니다.

____.

② 기다려 주셔서 감사합니다, 즐거운 비행 되십시오.

____.

③ 좌석번호 확인을 위해 탑승권을 볼 수 있을까요?

____.

2. 다음 문장을 한국어로 바꾸어 보세요.

① That seat is supposed to be my seat. However, it is already occupied.

____.

② I am sorry, but I am afraid that your seat is behind this seat.

____.

③ Here is some space for you. You can stow your bag here.

____

Situation

How would you deal with the situation if the passenger is sitting in a wrong seat?

Your Action

____.

____.

____.

INTERVIEW QUESTIONS

Question 1

Why do you have to check all carry-on items to be stored properly?

Answer 1

____.

____.

항공 서비스 영어

직무설명

이륙 전 지상서비스 업무

객실승무원은 모든 승객 탑승 후 이륙 전 기내에서 제공되는 지상 서비스를 실시하여야 한다. 이륙 전 지상 서비스는 항공사와 클래스 별로 다소 상이하다.

Unit 3

Ground Service
이륙 전 지상서비스

Vocabulary

No.	English	Korean
1	newspaper	신문
2	blanket	담요
3	pillow	베개
4	headphone(headset)	헤드셋
5	amenity kit	어메니티 키트
6	child kit	어린이용품
7	baby item	유아용품
8	RPA: restricted passenger advice	운송 제한 승객
9	Blind passenger	시각 장애인 승객
10	VIP(Very Important Person)	특별한 관심을 갖고 환대해야 할 고객
11	CIP(Commercially Important Person)	상업 상 주요 고객
12	FFP(Frequent-Flyer Program) Customer	회사 상용 고객

Practical Expression

1. Greeting VIP, CIP, FFP customer

Mr. / Mrs. /Ms. /Dr.

2. Providing ground service items

Would you like to read a newspaper?
to have a baby bassinet after take-off?
a headset?
Amenity kit?

This is a headset for you.
Here is your newspaper.

I'll get you one right away.

DIALOGUE

SITUATION 1 Greeting VIP, CIP, FFP customer

C: Excuse me, Mr. Kim. May I have your time a little bit?

P: Okay.

C: Good morning. Welcome aboard, Mr. Kim. My name is Stella and I will look after you on this flight.
If you need anything during the flight, please let me know.
Have a pleasant flight.

P: Thanks.

C: My Pleasure.

SITUATION 2 Providing Ground Service(Newspaper Service)

Would you like to read a newspaper?

I want to read New York Times.

I am sorry, but all New York Times are already taken. I will get you it right away once it is available.

Okay.

Thank you for your understanding.

SITUATION 3 Providing Ground Service(blanket)

Excuse me, I want to have one more blanket?

Definitely, sir. I'll get you one right now.

Thanks.

This is a blanket for you.
Do you need anything else, sir?

No, thank you.

If you need anything during the flight, please let me know.

SITUATION 4 Assisting Special Handling Customer(Blind Passenger)

Good afternoon, Welcome onboard. I am a cabin crew member on this flight. May I assist you with your seat?

Yes, please.

This is your seat, sir. I will also bring a safety instruction card in braille.

Okay.

Thank you for waiting. This is a safety instruction card. There are 2 toilets in the back of the cabin, and we will start lunch service after take-off.

You are so kind. Thanks a lot.

You're welcome. There is a call bell on the screen. If you need any assistance, please let me know.

Situation 1. Greeting VIP, CIP, FFP customer

Situation 2. Providing Ground Service

FILL IN THE BLANK

1. Thank you for your ______________.

2. I'll ______________ you it right now.

3. ______________ a blanket for you.

MATCH

A. Excuse me, I want to have one more blanket? •	• 1. My name is Stella and I will look after you on this flight.
B. Would you like to read a newspaper? •	• 2. I want to read New York Times.
C. Good morning. Welcome aboard, Mr. Kim. •	• 3. Definitely, ma'am. I'll get you one right now.

TRANSLATE BETWEEN KOREAN AND ENGLISH

1. 다음 문장을 영어로 바꾸어 보세요.

❶ 신문 읽으시겠습니까?

______________________________.

❷ 죄송합니다만, New Times는 이미 다 가져가셨습니다.

______________________________.

❸ 이해해 주셔서 감사합니다.

______________________________.

2. 다음 문장을 한국어로 바꾸어 보세요

❶ If you need anything during the flight, please let me know.

______________________________.

❷ Do you need anything else, sir?

______________________________.

❸ Good morning. Welcome aboard, Mr. Kim. My name is Stella and I will look after you on this flight.

______________________________.

ROLE PLAY

Situation

A passenger wants to have one more pillow, what would you do?

Your Action

______________________________.

______________________________.

______________________________.

INTERVIEW QUESTIONS

Question 1

What are the responsibilities as cabin crew during ground service?

Answer 1

______________________________.

______________________________.

직무설명

항공기 이륙 전 안전 및 보안 점검 업무

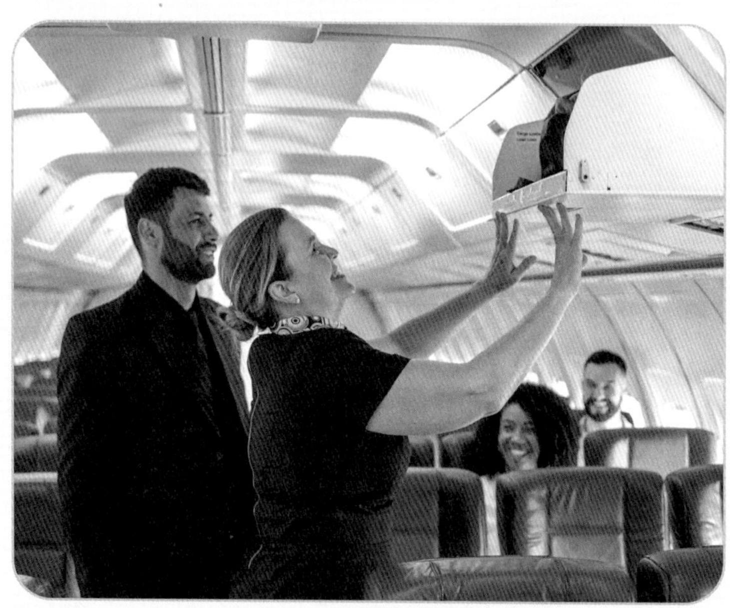

승무원은 이륙 준비를 위해 담당구역별로 객실 안전규정에 따라 승객 좌석, 객실 및 갤리의 안전 점검 사항을 재확인한다.

Unit 4

Preparation for take-off
이륙 준비

Vocabulary

No.	English	Korean
1	seatbelt	좌석벨트
2	tray table	트레이 테이블
3	window shades	창문 덮개
4	seatback	좌석 등받이
5	electronic devices	전자기기
6	take-off	이륙
7	Safety Regulation	안전 규정
8	fasten	(좌석벨트) 매다
9	turbulence	난기류
10	safety instruction card	안전 안내 카드
11	seat pocket	좌석 주머니

Practical Expression

1. Preparation for take-off

Please fasten your seatbelt for take-off.
close your tray table
open your window shades
return your seatback in the upright position.

All customers are required to fasten the seatbelt for take-off.
all tray table must be closed for take-off.
all window shades should be opened for safety reason.

Thank you for your cooperation.
Thank you for your understanding.

DIALOGUE

Cabin Crew

passenger

SITUATION 1 Preparation for take-off(Seatbelt)

C: Excuse me, sir. Please fasten your seatbelt for take-off.

P: It's okay.

C: All customers are required to fasten the seatbelt for take-off.
I request you fasten the seatbelt.

P: All right.

C: Thank you for your cooperation.

SITUATION 2 Preparation for take-off(Tray table)

Excuse me, sir. Would you please close your tray table for take-off?

I need to open my tray table.

Sir, all tray table must be closed for take-off.
You can open your tray table after take-off.

okay.

Thank you for your understanding.

SITUATION 3 Preparation for take-off(Window Shades)

Excuse me, ma'am. Please open your window shades.

No, I want to sleep while closing it.

Ma'am, all window shades should be opened for safety reason.
You can close your window shades after take-off.

okay.

Thank you for your cooperation.

GROUP ACTIVITY

Take turns practicing role-playing with your partners.

Situation 1. Preparation for take-off(Seatbelt)

Situation 2. Preparation for take-off(Tray table)

1. Please ____________ your seatbelt for take-off

2. Please ____________ your tray table for take-off?

3. Please ____________ your window shades.

MATCH

A. All customers are required to fasten •	• 1. the seatbelt for take-off.
B. Excuse me, Sir. All tray table •	• 2. must be closed for take-off.
C. Ma'am, all window shades •	• 3. should be opened for safety reason.

TRANSLATE BETWEEN KOREAN AND ENGLISH

1. 다음 문장을 영어로 바꾸어 보세요.

① 좌석벨트를 매 주십시오.

______________________________.

② 이해해 주셔서 감사합니다.

______________________________.

③ 이륙을 위해 테이블을 접어 주시겠습니까?

______________________________.

2. 다음 문장을 한국어로 바꾸어 보세요

① All tray table must be closed for take-off.

______________________________.

② All window shades should be opened for safety reason.

______________________________.

③ You can open your tray table after take-off.

______________________________.

ROLE PLAY

Situation

What would you do if a passenger doesn't want to fasten the seatbelt?

Your Action

____.

____.

____.

INTERVIEW QUESTIONS

Question 1

What are the qualifications required as cabin crew for preparation for take-off?

Answer 1

____.

____.

Chapter 2

In-flight Service

비행 중 서비스

Airline Services English

직무설명

비행 중 객실승무원의 업무

기내 서비스 준비 및 안내 방송

이륙 후, 안전벨트 표시등(Seatbelt sign)이 꺼지면 승무원은 자리에서 일어나 기내 서비스 준비를 위해 담당업무를 시작한다. 또한, 기내방송 담당 승무원은 좌석벨트 상시 착용 안내 방송을 실시한다.

기내 식음료 제공하기

항공사별 식음료 서비스 규정에 따라 특별식을 포함한 기내 식음료 서비스를 수행한다. 이코노미 객실의 경우 일반적으로 Meal service cart나 Meal tray로 제공된다.
동시에 식사 시간대에 따라 주류, 커피/차, 기타 음료를 제공한다. 비즈니스 객실 또는 퍼스트 클래스 객실의 경우 식기를 사용하며 주로 일대일 서비스 형태로 제공된다.

기내 오락물 제공하기

항공기별 기내 오락 기기의 종류에 차이가 있다. 개별 스크린이 있을 경우, 승객이 직접 리모콘 조작 또는 터치 스크린을 이용하여 영화, 드라마, 게임 등과 같은 기내 오락 시설을 즐기며, 중앙 통제 스크린의 경우 승무원이 정해진 영상물을 송출하면, 승객은 오디오 서비스만 이용 가능하다.

기내 면세품 판매하기

기내 면세품 판매 시작 전, 기내 면세품 판매 안내 방송을 한 뒤 Cart에 면세품을 진열하고 기내 전체를 순회하며 구매를 원하거나 사전예약주문한 승객에게 판매 또는 물품 전달을 한다. 주로 식음료 서비스 전 또는 후에 시행하며 일부 기내 면세품 판매를 하지 않는 항공사도 있다.
*기내 면세 판매 여부는 항공사에 따라 상이함

입국서류 배포하기

기내 서비스 종료 전과 후 또는 하기 전, 승무원은 승객에게 입국 시 요구되는 입국 서류(입국/세관 신고서, 검역 질문지 등)를 배포하고, 작성에 필요한 정보를 제공한다.

객실 상태 점검하기

객실 서비스 규정에 따라, 전 기내를 순회하며 기내 청결 상태를 확인하고, 적정 온도 및 조도를 유지 및 관리한다.
또한, 기내 통로 및 비상구 주변에 장애물이 있는지 확인하는 등 승객의 안전과 쾌적한 휴식을 위해 지속적으로 기내 모니터링을 실시한다.

Unit 1

In-flight Bar & Meal Service

기내 식음료 서비스 제공하기

No.	English	Korean
1	Food and Beverages(F&B)	식음료
2	meal tray	(주로 이코노미 객실의) 기내식 트레이
3	cutlery	(나이프, 포크 따위의) 날붙이류, 커틀러리
4	appetizer / amuse-bouche	전채, 에피타이저
5	main dish	메인 요리
6	condiment	(음식의) 양념, 소스
7	special meal	특별식
8	alcoholic beverages	주류
9	mocktail	알코올이 없는 칵테일
10	garnish	(음료 및 음식 위에 얹는) 가니쉬, 고명, 장식
11	aperitif	(식사 전에 식욕을 돋우는) 식전주
12	digestif	(식사 후 소화는 돕기 위해 마시는) 식후주
13	soft drinks	청량음료
14	fizzy drinks	탄산음료

Practical Expression

1. During bar & meal service

Would you care for something to **drink?**
eat?

Would you like to have **a cup of coffee/tea?**
something else?
another glass of wine?
one more drink?

Would you like to join us for **breakfast?**
Will you join us for **brunch**
lunch
dinner

2. During tray collection & clearance

Are you **finished?**
done with your meal/main dish/dessert?

(And then)

May I **clean your table?**
collect your meal tray?(Mainly in Economy service)

DIALOGUE

After take-off, the cabin crew is about to start the bar & meal service. Prior to starting the service, all cabin crew members should be aware of the details of bar items, meal choices, and special meal orders accordingly.

SITUATION 1 Conducting a bar service

C: Good afternoon!
Would you care for something to drink?

P: Yes, please. What kind of drinks do you have?

C: We have a wide range of drinks such as soft drinks, fruit juices, champagne, wine, beer, vodka, cognac and so on.

P: Do you serve any cocktails on board?

C: Yes, of course. There are various cocktails available on board. We also can mix your favorite cocktail if you like.

P: Oh, that's great! I'll have a gin and tonic with ice and a lemon slice.

C: Certainly, sir.

SITUATION 2 Conducting a meal service

Good evening! Would you like to join us for dinner?

Yes, please. What do you have?

We do have Chicken breast with mixed vegetables, Braised beef with mashed potatoes, and Stir-fried noodle for vegetarian customers.

I'll have the Chicken option, please.

Here you are. Please enjoy your dinner, ma'am.

Thank you.

SITUATION 3 Serving a special meal order

Hello, Ma'am. Are you Ms. Fatima?

Yes, I am.

Great! You've requested for a Low Sodium meal, right?

Yes, I did.

Okay, here's your Low Sodium meal. Would you like to have any drinks along with your meal?

Sure, I'd like to have a glass of Coke Zero without ice.

Alright, here you are.

SITUATION 4 A shortage of meal choices

Sir, would you like to eat something? We're currently doing the meal service.

Yes, please.

Have you seen the menu card? we have 3 meal choices.

Yes, I did. I'd like to have the Beef option.

I'm sorry, but I'm afraid that we are running out of that option today.

Hm... What else do you have then?

Apart from a Beef choice, all other choices are available now.

Okay, I'll take the Cubed Chicken with cream sauce.

Excellent choice, sir! Please enjoy your meal. Is there anything else that I can offer you?

No, I'm fine, Thank you.

You're welcome.
And I really appreciate your kind understanding.

SITUATION 5 Meal Tray Collection & Clearance

May I collect your meal tray if you're done with it?

Yes, you may.

Would you like to have a cup of tea or coffee?

I'll have a cup of coffee with two sugar tubes, please.

Here you are.

Take turns practicing role-playing with your partners.

Situation 1. Conducting a bar and meal service

Situation 2. Serving a special meal order

Situation 3. A shortage of meal choices

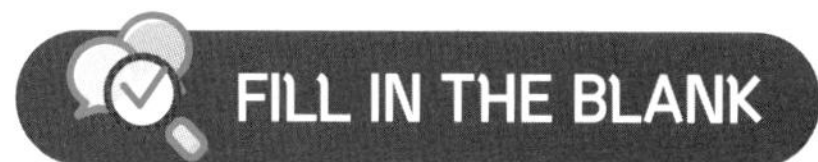

mix　　afraid　　appreciate

1. We also can ____________ your favorite cocktail if you like.

2. I'm sorry, but I'm ____________ that we are running out of that menu today.

3. I really ____________ your kind understanding.

MATCH

A. Would you like to •	• 1. drink something?
B. Enjoy your meal. •	• 2. Certainly.
C. I'll have Chicken. •	• 3. Thank you.
D. Do you serve alcohol? •	• 4. Excellent choice!
E. Coffee, please. •	• 5. Yes, we do.

TRANSLATE BETWEEN KOREAN AND ENGLISH

1. 다음 문장을 영어로 바꾸어 보세요.

① 음료 드시겠습니까?

____.

② 원하신다면 좋아하는 칵테일을 만들어 드릴 수 있습니다.

____.

③ 죄송하지만, 유감스럽게도 해당 메뉴는 지금 다 떨어졌습니다.

____.

2. 다음 문장을 한국어로 바꾸어 보세요

① We have a wide range of drinks.

____.

② Is there anything else I can offer you?

____.

③ May I collect your meal tray if you are finished with your meal?

____.

Situation

What would you do if an economy class customer asks for a First-class meal?

Your Action

____.

____.

____.

INTERVIEW QUESTIONS

Question 1

What are the cabin crew duties after take-off?

Answer 1

____.

____.

Question 2

How would you conduct the meal service to passengers?

Answer 2

____.

____.

Unit 2

In-flight Entertainment

기내 오락서비스 제공하기

Vocabulary of In-flight Service

No.	English	Korean
1	In-flight entertainment (=IFE) system	기내 오락 시스템
2	VOD (Video-On-Demand) system	주문형 비디오 시스템
3	headset/headphone	헤드폰
4	Handset (=remote control)	(텔레비전 등의) 리모컨
5	In-flight magazine	기내 잡지
6	movie program	영화 프로그램
7	Inoperative (=INOP)	작동하지 않는
8	malfunction	제대로 작동하지 않다
9	sound system	음향 장치
10	genre	(예술 작품의) 장르
11	sci-fi movie	SF영화, 공상과학 영화
12	documentary	다큐멘터리
13	romantic movie	로맨틱 영화

Practical Expression

1. When passenger asks for help

Do you need help?

How may I help you?

May I help you?

Is there anything I can do for you?

What can I do for you?

2. Other Useful Expressions

We are sorry for ~

We apologize for ~

We thank you for ~ .

We appreciate ~ .

DIALOGUE

The passenger enjoys playing IFE system in each seat during the flight. But certain situations could occur at this time, for instance, IFE system malfunction, defective headset or asking how to use them.

SITUATION 1 A passenger asks for help

P: Excuse me.

C: Yes, sir. How may I help you?

P: I don't know how to play this handset.

C: No worries, let me show you how to use it.

P: Where should I connect this headphone?

C: There is a connection right next to the screen.

P: Oh, I found it. Thank you so much!

SITUATION 2 The headset is inoperative

Excuse me.

I can't hear the sound. Maybe there's a problem with this headset.

Oh, we're so sorry about that. Let me change it for you.

(*After a while*)

Thank you for your patience. Here you go. Please try this.

Oh, it's working now. Thank you.

You're welcome.

Please feel free to let us know if you need anything.

Okay, thank you so much.

SITUATION 3 IFE system malfunction

Excuse me, my screen is not working. The screen won't turn on.

Let me check the screen first, sir.

Okay.

I'm sorry, sir. I think I'd better reset the IFE system in your seat. It will take about 15 minutes. Would you mind waiting for a while?
Please do not touch the screen and use the handset during that time.
Meanwhile, should I get some magazines or newspapers for you?

No, I'm fine.

(*After about 15 minutes*)

Thank you for waiting, sir. Could you try to play the movie again?

Oh, it's working now. Thank you.

You're most welcome. Please let us know at any time if it's not working again.

Take turns practicing role-playing with your partners.

Situation 1. The headset is not working

Situation 2. IFE system is inoperative

free patience reset

1. Please feel ______________ to let us know if it's not working again.

2. Thank you for your ______________.

3. I think I'd better ______________ the IFE system in your seat.

MATCH

A. I don't know •

B. Thank you for •

C. Where should I •

D. Would you prefer to •

E. Excellent choice! •

• 1. connect this head-phone?

• 2. how to play this handset.

• 3. pay by credit card?

• 4. your waiting

• 5. Thank you.

TRANSLATE BETWEEN KOREAN AND ENGLISH

1. 다음 문장을 영어로 바꾸어 보세요.

① 제가 리모컨 사용법을 알려드리겠습니다.

______________________________.

② 제 스크린이 고장났습니다.

______________________________.

③ 영화를 다시 한 번 재생해보시겠습니까?

______________________________.

2. 다음 문장을 한국어로 바꾸어 보세요

① There is a connection right next to the screen.

______________________________.

② Where should I connect this headphone?

______________________________.

③ Let me reset the IFE system for you, ma'am.

______________________________.

Situation

How would you deal with the situation if the passenger told you that the headphone is not working?

Your Action

____.

____.

____.

Question 1

If the customer complains about the limited movie selections, what will you do?

Answer 1

____.

____.

Unit 3

In-flight Duty-Free sales
기내 면세품 판매하기

Vocabulary of In-flight Service

No.	English	Korean
1	pre-order	사전예약주문
2	In-flight duty-free sales	기내 면세품 판매
3	debit card	체크카드
4	credit card	신용카드
5	call bell	(객실에서 승무원을 부를 때 사용하는) 벨
6	payment	지불
7	cosmetic	화장품
8	perfume	향수
9	fragrance	향기, 향
10	currency	통화
11	exchange rate	환전
12	carton	한갑

Practical Expression

1. During In-flight Duty-free Sales

Would you like to join for	duty-free shopping?
Are you interested in	

Would you like to	buy	some duty-free	items?
	Purchase		goods
	Order		products

2. Other useful expressions

Would you like to purchase any duty-free items?

Is this the one you are looking for?

The item is currently out of stock.

DIALOGUE

Before or after the meal service, the duty-free service is conducted. But not all airline companies have the in-flight duty-free sales on board.

SITUATION 1 During duty-free sales

C: Would you like to purchase any duty-free items?

P: Yes, I'd like to buy this perfume.

C: Certainly, ma'am. Would you prefer to pay cash or by credit card?

P: I'll pay by credit card.

C: Please wait a second. Here is your product with a receipt. Again, thank you for the purchase.

SITUATION 2 When there're pre-order duty-free items

Excuse me.

Yes, sir. May I help you?

I pre-ordered duty-free items few days ago. Can I have it?

Certainly, sir! Let me quickly check the pre-order items.

(*After a while*)

Thank you for waiting. You've ordered a bracelet, item No. 5334B. Is it correct?

Yes, that's the one I ordered.

Excellent choice! Here you are. We hope you would like the item.

Thank you.

SITUATION 3 When the item is not available

I'd like to buy cigarette. Do you have Marlboro Red?

Let me check for you, sir.
I'm so sorry, but I'm afraid that the Marlboro Red is out of stock in this flight. But we do have Marlboro Gold.

How come all the flights don't have Marlboro Red?

Really? I feel so sorry about that.
There were a few of them left earlier in this flight. But other passengers bought all of them right before you. So, it's sold out now.

Okay, I should try again on my next flight.

Thank you for your understanding.

Take turns practicing role-playing with your partners.

Situation 1. During duty-free sales

Situation 2. When the duty-free item is not available

REARRANGE THE GIVEN WORDS

a receipt　product　is　here　your　with

1. ______________________________.

There　in　a few　of　them　this　were　earlier
left　flight.

2. ______________________________.

MATCH

A. I'll pay •	• 1. Certainly, sir.
B. I should try again •	• 2. by credit card.
C. Can I have my items? •	• 3. the item is out of stock
D. I'm so sorry, but I'm afraid •	• 4. on my next flight.

TRANSLATE BETWEEN KOREAN AND ENGLISH

1. 다음 문장을 영어로 바꾸어 보세요.

① 여기 제품과 영수증이 있습니다.

____.

② 구매해 주셔서 감사합니다.

____.

③ 현재 그 제품은 재고가 없습니다.

____.

2. 다음 문장을 한국어로 바꾸어 보세요

① Would you prefer to pay cash or by credit card?

____.

② I pre-ordered Duty-Free items few days ago.

____.

③ it's sold out at this moment.

____.

Situation

A passenger wants to buy cigarettes, but the item is out of stock.

Your Action

____.

____.

____.

Question 1

If the duty-free item that a passenger is looking for is unavailable in flight, what will you do?

Answer 1

____.

____.

____.

항공 서비스 영어

Unit 4

Distribution of CQI documents & Walk Around

입국서류 배포하기 및 객실 상태 점검하기

Vocabulary of In-flight Service

No.	English	Korean
1	entry documents	입국 서류
2	customs (declaration) form	세관 신고서
3	Quarantine	검역
4	Immigration form	출입국 신고서
5	Landing/arrival card	입국 신고서
6	fill out	작성하다
7	exceed	초과하다
8	transit	경유하다
9	one per family	가족 당 하나
10	ESTA	미국 관광 비자
11	passport holder	여권 소지자
12	cabin patrol	기내 순찰

Practical Expression

1. During Landing Documents Distribution

Please fill out the customs/immigration forms.

Are you a Korean/American/European passport holder?

Are you traveling alone or with your family?

Do you have anything to declare?

Passengers must declare all goods purchased abroad.

Meat products are strictly prohibited when entering EU countries.

DIALOGUE

Prior to landing, the cabin crew distributes CQI forms such as Customs Declaration Form, Landing(Entry) card, and Quarantine.

SITUATION 1 Distribution of CQI forms

C: Here is the customs form. Please fill out before landing.

P: Okay, can I borrow a pen?

C: I'm sorry, I already lent other passengers.
Once they return to me, I'll give it to you.

P: All right, no problem.

SITUATION 2 Response for Inquiries

Excuse me.

Yes, ma'am. How may I assist you?

I'm travelling with my family, and I don't know how to fill out this form. Can you help me with this?

Sure, May I see your passport and boarding pass?

Here it is.

(*A while later*)

It's done ma'am. Are you travelling alone or with a family?

I'm travelling with my parents.

Then, you need to fill out this form only since the customs form is one per family.

I see, thank you so much for your help.

SITUATION 3 Shortage of CQI forms

Excuse me. Could I have another landing card? I made a mistake.

Unfortunately, we have no more extra landing cards in this flight.

Then, what should I do?

You don't need to worry about it, sir. There are landing cards in the arrivals area. So, you can fill out the form there, too.

Okay, I'll do that.

DIALOGUE

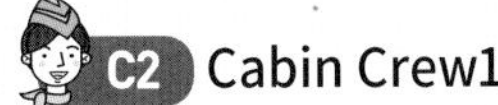

SITUATION 4 Walk around the cabin

(*Conversation between cabin crews*)

I'll go and walk around the cabin to ensure everything is okay.

Thanks. Just be careful, it's quite dark as we dimmed the lights in the cabin.

(*During walk around, cabin crew found many passengers were standing at the door area*)

I'm sorry to interrupt you all. But, for safety reasons, the area near emergency exits must be kept clear throughout the flight.
So, please return to your seat or stay in another area.

Take turns practicing role-playing with your partners.

Situation 1. Response for inquiries

Situation 2. Shortage of CQI forms

FILL IN THE BLANK

fill out　　customs form　　landing card

1. I don't know how to ______________ this form.

2. the ______________ is one per family

3. There are ______________ in the airport.

MATCH

A. How may I •

B. You don't need to •

C. I don't know •

D. May I see your •

E. The exit area •

• 1. assist you?

• 2. how to fill out this form.

• 3. worry about it.

• 4. must be kept clear.

• 5. passport and boarding pass?

TRANSLATE BETWEEN KOREAN AND ENGLISH

1. 다음 문장을 영어로 바꾸어 보세요.

① 이미 다른 승객분께 빌려드렸습니다.

______________________________.

② 당신의 여권과 탑승권을 볼 수 있을까요?

______________________________.

③ 공항에도 입국신고서가 있습니다.

______________________________.

2. 다음 문장을 한국어로 바꾸어 보세요

① May I see your passport and boarding pass?

______________________________.

② Could I have another landing card?

______________________________.

③ For safety reasons, the exit area must be kept clear throughout the flight.

______________________________.

ROLE PLAY

Situation

What would you do if there's no more landing card left?

Your Action

____.

____.

____.

INTERVIEW QUESTIONS

Question 1

Tell me what you know about cabin crew duties before landing.

Answer 1

____.

____.

Chapter 3

Preparation for landing 착륙준비

Airline Services English

직무설명

 **Cabin crew duty before landing**(착륙 전 승무원의 업무)

기장의 TOD 방송

착륙 30분전 기장은 착륙안내 방송을 실시하고 승무원들은 착륙 전 업무를 실시한다.

*top of decent: 최고 하강점

방해요소 물품 회수

승무원은 착륙에 방해될 수 있는 요소인 헤드셋과 담요, 남아 있던 컵들을 회수한다.

객실 및 갤리 안전점검

객실과 갤리 포함 기내의 안전 점검을 실시하고 화장실을 사용중인 승객이 있는지 점검하며 착륙을 위해 착석을 요청한다.

객실 머리 위 선반 및 갤리 내의 카트, 컨테이너 등의 안전장치 잠금 여부를 점검한다.

기내 안전 최종 확인

승객의 착석 및 트레이 테이블, 팔걸이, 머리 위 선반, 안전벨트 착용여부 및 승객 가방 위치 등을 최종확인 한다.

이때 객실 비상 탈출구 주변 및 통로 주변에 장애물 여부를 확인한다.

Unit 1

Preparation for landing
착륙준비

Vocabulary of In-flight Service

No.	English	Korean
1	Cooperation	협조
2	Window shade	창문 가리개
3	Armrest	비행기나 자동차 좌석의 팔걸이
4	Overhead bin	여객기 객석 위에 있는 짐 넣는 곳
5	Aisle	통로, 복도
6	Secure	안전하게 지키다, 단단히 보안장치를 하다.
7	Baby bassinet	항공기 객실 앞의 벽면에 설치하여 사용하는 기내용 유아 요람
8	Stow	(안전한곳에) 집어넣다.
9	Seatback	의자 뒷부분
10	Upright	수직으로 똑바로 세워 둔
11	Afterwards	나중에, 그 뒤에

1. During securing the cabin

Could you please	put your bag under the seat in front of you
	open your window shades for landing.
	fasten your seatbelt?
Would you please	put your bag in the overhead bin?
	return to your seat we will be landing shortly.
	put your seatback to the up-right position?
	stow your tray table?

2. Collecting stuff from passenger

May I take	**a baby bassinet for landing**
	headsets?
	your mug?
	blanket?

DIALOGUE

SITUATION 1 During headsets collection

C: Excuse me sir, may I take your headsets for landing?

P: Can I Keep it please? I would love to finish watching this movie

C: Certainly sir. When you leave the aircraft, just put them on the seat please.

P: I will do it. Thank you so much!

C: You're very welcome.

SITUATION 2 During final clearance

Excuse me ma'am. Are you done with your coffee?

Yes, I am done.

May I take your mug please?

Yes, you can take it. Thank you so much

My pleasure. Could you please stow your tray table for landing?

Okay!

SITUATION 3 Asking passenger to return to his/her seat for landing

Excuse me sir, would you please return to your seat?
We will be landing shortly.

I want to use the lavatory please.

I am afraid we will be landing soon sir.
You can use it afterwards.

Okay.

SITUATION 4 Securing cabin for landing(1)

Excuse me, would you please put your seat back to the upright position?

Okay.

Thank you. Please open your window shades for landing as well.

I will.

SITUATION 5 Securing cabin for landing(2)

Excuse me ma'am. Could you please remove your bag from aisle and put it under the seat in front of you for landing?

Why? Can't I leave them here?

I am afraid that aisle has to be clear for the safety reason ma'am.

I see. I will put them under the seat.

And please put your armrest down and fasten your seat-belt as well.

Okay. I will.

take, afterwards, upright, shortly, in front of

1. Could you please return to your seat? We will be landing ___________.

2. Would you please put your bag under the seat ___________ you?

3. Are you done with your coffee? May I ___________ your mug please?

4. Could you please put your seatback to the ___________ position?

5. I am afraid we will be landing soon sir. You can use it ___________.

MATCH

A. Sir could you please return to your seat? We will be landing shortly. •

B. Please open your window shades for landing •

C. May I take your headsets for landing please? •

D. Could you please stow your tray table for landing? •

E. Are you done with your coffee? May I take your mug? •

• 1. Sir could you please return to your seat? We will be landing shortly.

• 2. Please open your window shades for landing

• 3. May I take your headsets for landing please?

• 4. Could you please stow your tray table for landing?

• 5. Are you done with your coffee? May I take your mug?

TRANSLATE BETWEEN KOREAN AND ENGLISH

1. 다음 문장을 영어로 바꾸어 보세요.

❶ 손님 자리로 돌아가 주시겠습니까?

____.

❷ 저희는 곧 착륙 합니다.

____.

❸ 착륙을 위해 좌석벨트를 매주시기 바랍니다.

____.

2. 다음 문장을 한국어로 바꾸어 보세요.

❶ Please open your window shades for landing.

____.

❷ I am afraid we will be landing shortly, you can use it afterwards.

____.

❸ Could you please put your armrest down for landing?

____.

Situation

1. What would you do if your passenger refuses to return to his/her seat?

Your Action

____.

2. We are about to be landing soon. What would say if your passenger asks to use lavatory?

Your Action

____.

GROUP ACTIVITY

① Explain to your passenger who wants to know why the aisle has to be clear for landing.

② Ask passenger to fasten seatbelt for landing.

③ Collect blanket, headsets, mug from passenger for landing.

④ Securing the cabin. (seat up right, remove the bag from aisle, armrest, etc.)

직무설명

Cabin crew duty after landing(착륙 후 승무원 업무)

기장의 도착 안내 방송 및 환송방송

기장의 목적지 도착 안내방송 이후 승무원이 환송/페어웰 방송을 하며 이때 승객안전을 위해 좌석벨트등 사인이 꺼질 때까지 착석유지를 당부한다.

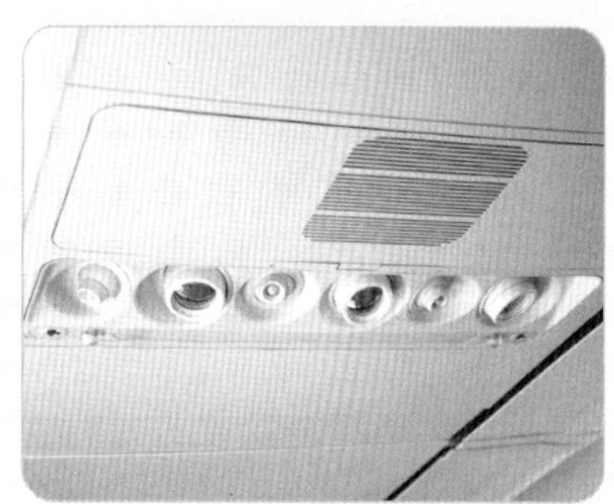

택싱중 안전업무

비행기가 완전히 멈추지 않았는데 일어나 오버헤드빈에서 짐을 꺼내거나 돌아다니는 승객이 있다면 좌석벨트등 사인이 꺼질 때까지 착석 당부 요청 기내방송을 한다. 이때 승무원은 담당 구역내의 승객들에게 다시 한번 착석을 요청한다.

담당 구역 도어 오픈

비행기가 완전히 멈춘 후 승무원은 담당 구역 도어의 슬라이드 표시를 정상 위치로 바꾼 후 반대편의 승무원과 확인한다. 사무장은 기내 모든 도어의 슬라이드 표시가 정상일 때 문을 열수 있게 지시한다.

환송인사

승무원은 담당구역에서 승객에게 환송인사를 드리고 승객 하기 시 원활하게 진행되도록 돕는다. 휠체어가 필요한 승객이나 UM등 에게 필요한 도움을 준다.

*UM - Unaccompanied minor 동반자 없는 어린이승객

Unit 2

Cabin crew duty after landing
착륙 후 승무원 업무

Vocabulary of Cabin crew duty after landing

No.	English	Korean
1	Safety	안전
2	Departure board	출발 안내 전광판
3	Switch off	스위치를 끄기
4	Remain	남다
5	Wheelchair	휠체어
6	Unaccompanied minor	보호자 없이 혼자 항공편을 이용하는 어린이 승객
7	Seated	앉는
8	Completely	완전히
9	Manage	(힘든 일을) 해내다
10	Enjoy	즐거운 시간을 보내다

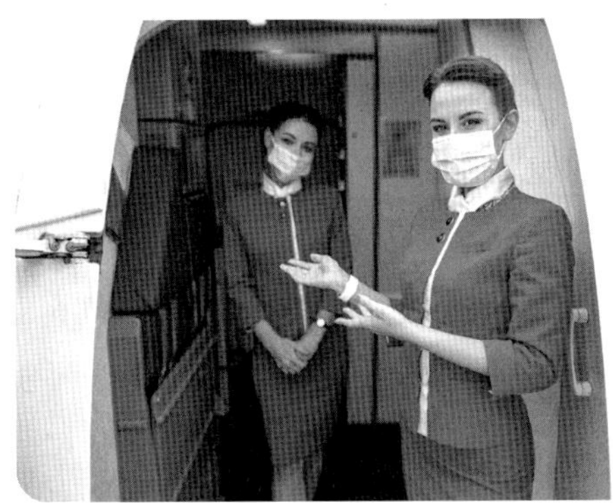

1. During taxing

Could you please take your seat until the seatbelt sign is switched off?

Would you please remain seated?

2. During farewell

Did you enjoy your flight?

I hope to see you again soon.

Thank you so much for flying with us.

DIALOGUE

SITUATION 1 Asking passenger to remain seated

C: Excuse me sir, the seatbelt sign is still on. Could you please remain seated?

P: Oh sorry!

C: It is okay. For your safety, please seated until the aircraft is completely stops.

P: Okay I understand.

SITUATION 2 Assisting passenger with baggage

Could you please help me to get my bag?

Certainly. Which one is your ma'am?

The pink one on the right side please

There you go! Can you manage?

I got it. Thank you so much!

My pleasure!

SITUATION 3 During farewell

Did you enjoy your flight?

I did. It was wonderful! Thank you so much for your service.

I am glad to hear that. I hope to see you again soon.

SITUATION 4 Answering about connecting flight

Excuse me, where can I check the gate for my next flight?

You can check at the departure board outside sir.

OH, thank you. I hope I won't miss my next flight.

Let me check the time for your next flight. You have enough time sir don't worry!

Thank you so much!

FILL IN THE BLANK

remain, completely, seated, safety

1. For your ______________, please remain seated sir.

2. Please ______________ seated until the seatbelt sign has been switched off.

3. You are not supposed to stand up until the aircraft __________ stops.

4. Passengers are required to be ______________ for their safety.

A. Did you enjoy your flight? •

B. Could you please help me to get my bag? •

C. Please take your seat for your safety. •

D. Where can I check the gate for the next flight? •

E. It was such a nice flight. Thank you for the service. •

• 1. It was wonderful! Thank you.

• 2. Certainly. Where is yours?

• 3. Okay

• 4. You can check at the departure board.

• 5. Glad to hear that. I hope to see you soon!

TRANSLATE BETWEEN KOREAN AND ENGLISH

1. 다음 문장을 영어로 바꾸어 보세요.

❶ 손님 좌석벨트 등이 꺼질 때까지 앉아주세요.

______________________________.

❷ 비행은 어떠셨나요?

______________________________.

❸ 감사합니다. 곧 다시 뵙기를 바랍니다!

______________________________.

2. 다음 문장을 한국어로 바꾸어 보세요

❶ Where can I check the gate for the next flight?

______________________________.

❷ Could you please take your seat until the seatbelt sign has been switched off?

______________________________.

❸ Thank for flying with us. We hope to see you soon again.

______________________________.

ROLE PLAY

Situation

1. What would you do if your passenger is standing up when the aircraft is still moving?

Your Action

____.

____.

2. What would you say to passengers when they leave the aircraft?

Your Action

____.

____.

GROUP ACTIVITY

① Explain to your passenger who wants to know why they need to sit down.

② Ask passenger to sit down for the safety.

③ What does UM mean?

④ Say good bye to passengers when they leave the aircraft.

Question 1

What are the cabin crew duties after landing?

Answer 1

____.

____.

Question 2

Can passenger stand up during taxing?

Answer 2

____.

____.

직무설명

 **Post landing duties**(승객들 하기 후 승무원 업무)

담당구역의 객실 유실물 점검

모든 승객이 하기 후 객실 승무원은 UM이나 기내 휠체어가 필요한 승객들을 도운 후 담당구역의 객실 유실물 점검을 한다.

객실 유실물 처리

승객이 하기 후 자리에 물건을 놓고 내린 경우 좌석번호를 확인한 후 승무원이 직접 유실물을 가져다 준다.
보안정책상 승객은 하기 후 다시 비행기 내부에 들어올 수 없다.
습득한 유실물은 사무장에게 보고 후 사무장은 물건을 지상 직원에게 전달한다.

Unit 3 Post landing duties
승객들 하기 후 승무원의 업무

Post landing duties

No.	English	Korean
1	Lost and found	분실물 취급소
2	Security	보안
3	Seat pocket	좌석 앞 주머니
4	Disembark	(배나 비행기에서) 내리다
5	Re-enter	다시 들어가다
6	UM (unaccompanied minor)	동반자 없는 어린이 승객
7	Left behind	두고가다
8	Hand over	인도하다
9	Belongings	재산, 소유물
10	Valuables	귀중품

Practical Expression

1. During special care for passenger

Could you please wait until everyone leaves the aircraft?

Thank you for waiting. I will get you the wheelchair.

What is your seat number? I will find it for you.

Could you please remain seated? I will come and get you.

DIALOGUE

C Cabin Crew

P passenger

SITUATION 1 Dealing with passenger who wants to re-enter the aircraft

I left something behind on my seat. I want to go in again and get it.

What is your seat number? I will find it for you. For the security reason you can not re-enter the aircraft.

I was sitting on 45B.

Which item did you leave?

I left my portable charger in the seat pocket.

SITUATION 2 Assisting with on-board wheelchair

Excuse me, I need wheelchair.

Certainly Sir, when everyone disembarks the aircraft, I will get the wheelchair for you.

Okay. I will wait on my seat

Thank you for your understanding.

SITUATION 3 Assisting with wheelchair passenger

Excuse me, I need wheelchair at the airport.

Sir, after leave the aircraft the ground staff will assist you with wheelchair.

Okay. Where can I meet the ground staff?

He will be waiting for you outside of the aircraft near the door.

Thank you!

My pleasure!

DIALOGUE

Cabin Crew1

Cabin Crew2

passenger

SITUATION 4 Finding lost item in your zone

Has anyone found lost items in your zone?

I found one bag on 60C.

Okay. Anything else?

No. Only one bag was left behind.

Okay thank you. I will hand over to the ground staff.

My pleasure!

SITUATION 5 Having UM in your zone

You have UM in your zone. Please remind her to remain seated and keep an eye on her.

Okay. I will!
Could you please remain seated until everybody leaves the aircraft? I will come and get you.

Okay I will wait for you.

hand over, leaves, re-enter, left

1. Please remain seated until everybody ____________ the aircraft

2. For the security reason, you can't ____________ the aircraft.

3. I think I ____________ my wallet on my seat.

4. I will ____________ to the ground staff.

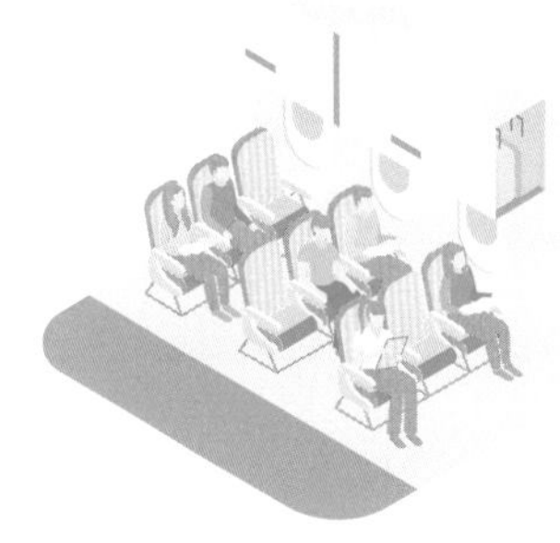

A. What is your seat number? •

B. I need wheelchair outside. •

C. Could you please remain seated until I come and get you? •

D. I want to go in to the aircraft again. •

E. Has anyone found lost items in your zone? •

• 1. ground staff will assist you.

• 2. I found one bag in my zone.

• 3. Okay. I will wait for you.

• 4. For the security reason you can not re-enter.

• 5. I was sitting 57F.

TRANSLATE BETWEEN KOREAN AND ENGLISH

1. 다음 문장을 영어로 바꾸어 보세요.

① 지상직원이 비행기 밖에서 도와드리겠습니다.

______________________________.

② 좌석번호가 어떻게 되시나요?

______________________________.

③ 어떤 물건을 두고 내리셨나요?

______________________________.

2. 다음 문장을 한국어로 바꾸어 보세요.

① I will hand over to the ground staff.

______________________________.

② Sir, when everyone disembarks the aircraft, I will get the wheelchair for you.

______________________________.

③ For the security reason, you can not re-enter the aircraft.

______________________________.

Situation

1. What would you do if your passenger wants to re-enter the aircraft?

Your Action

____.

____.

____.

2. What would you do if you found some items on passenger's seat?

Your Action

____.

____.

____.

GROUP ACTIVITY

① Ask passenger about the seat number and left behind item.

② Tell the UM to remain seated until a member of cabin crew come and get UM.

③ Inform the passenger that a ground staff will assist you with wheelchair.

INTERVIEW QUESTIONS

Question 1

What are the cabin crew duties after passenger disembarkation?

Answer 1

____.

____.

____.

Chapter 4

Safety and service issue

안전과 서비스 문제

Airline Services English

직무설명

기내 응급 의료상황 중 객실 승무원의 역할

기압의 변화로 승객의 건강상태에 영향을 주어기내에서는 의료상황이 발생할 수 있다.
객실 승무원은 기내에서 이용할 수 있는 응급처치법과의료장비의 종류와 그 위치를 정확히 알고 있어야 한다. 객실 승무원은 기내에서 승객의 건강을 담당하고 일차적인 응급처치하는 교육을 받고 있다.

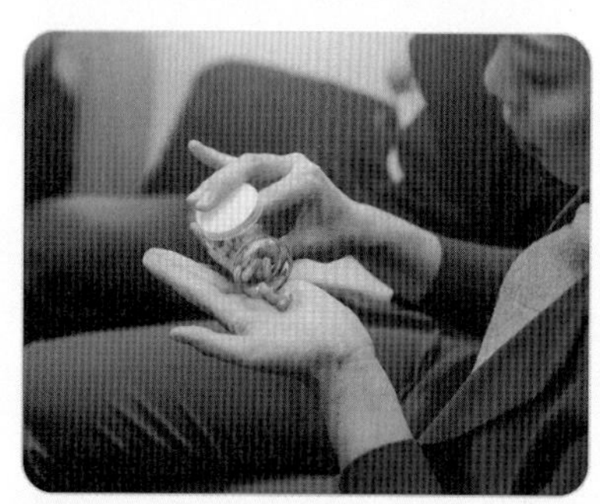

기내에서 발생할 수 있는 흔한 승객의 증상

두통 (headache), 감기 (cold), 인후통 (Sore throat)열(fever), 멀미 (Airsickness), 소화불량(Indigestion)호흡곤란(Shortness of breath), 천식(Asthma), 화상(burn), 구토(vomiting) 및 매스꺼움 (nausea설사(Diarrhea), 귀의 통증(Ear pain),복통(stomachache)

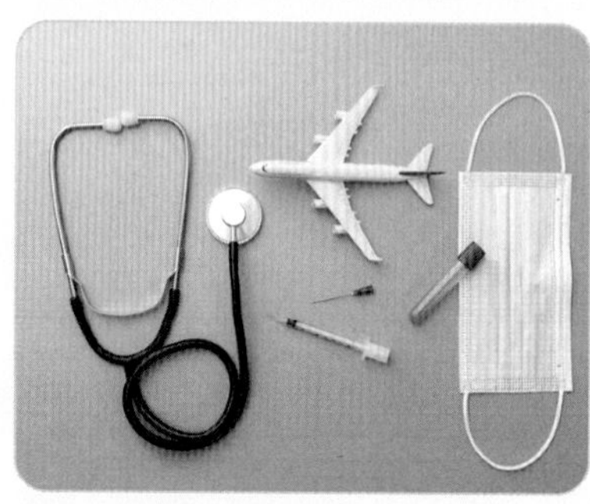

기내에서 의료 약품 제공 시 확인할 사항

- 약물에 대한 알레르기
- 알코올 섭취 여부
- (여성) 임신 여부

세 가지 사항을 의료 약품을 제공 전에 물어보고, 한가지라도 만족하지 않을 때는 약물 제공이 어려울 수 있다.

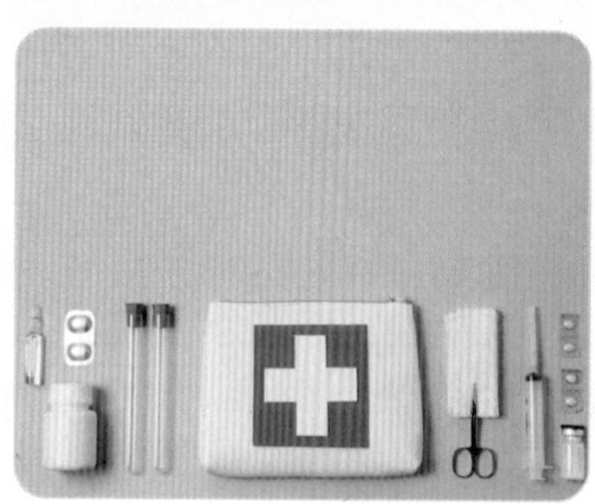

기내에 구비 된 의료장비들

객실 승무원은 일반적인 기내 응급상황에 대한 응급처치, 심폐소생술 및 AED 사용 교육을 받는다.

- 구급상자(First Aid Kit)
- 비상 구급상자(Emergency Medical Kit)
- 자동 심장 충격기(Automated External Defibrillator)
- 자동제세동기(AED), 휴대용 산소통(P02 Bottle)

In-flight Medical situation
기내 의료 사항

Vocabulary of In-flight Medical situation

No.	English	Korean
1	Headache	두통, 머리가 아픔
2	Medicine	약, 약물
3	Allergies	알레르기, 이상 과민증
4	At once	즉시, 동시에, 한꺼번에
5	Fever	열
6	Symptoms	증상, 증후
7	Catch a cold	감기에 들다, 감기에 걸리다
8	Helpful	도움이 되는, 기꺼이 돕는
9	Running nose	콧물
10	Cough	기침, 기침하다
11	Indigestion	소화불량
12	Dizzy	어지러운, 아찔한
13	Nauseous	메스꺼운, 역겨운
14	Airsickness bag	비행기 멀미용 위생 봉투

Practical Expression

May I ask some questions before I bring some medicine?
Can pills?

I 'll bring it to you right away.
soon.
shortly.
in a moment.

I hope you are feeling better.
feel better soon.
get well.

If there is anything I can do for you, just let me know
If you need anything else

I am sorry to hear that
happy

DIALOGUE

SITUATION 1 Sick passenger about Headache

P: Excuse me, I think I have a headache. Do you have any medicine for headaches? If so, can I have one?

C: Oh, I am so sorry to hear that Ma'am. Of course, we have a medicine for your headache. May I ask some questions before I bring some medicine?
Do you have any allergies to the medicine or Did you take any alcohol on a board?

P: No, I don't have any allergies and I did not take any wine or beer at all on board today.

C: Thank you for answering that nicely! I'll bring it to you right away.

(*After a while*)

C: Excuse me. Ma'am. Thank you for waiting. Here's your medicine and a glass of warm water. Please take two pills at once.

P: Okay, thank you

C: You're welcome. I hope you are feeling better.

SITUATION 2 Sick passenger about cold

Excuse me. I don't feel good today. I think I have a slight fever and body ache.
I think I need to have medicine.

Oh, I am sorry to hear that you are not feeling good.
May I ask that you have any other symptoms? like a runny nose or cough?

Not at the moment. I think I caught a cold.

Don't worry sir, we have a pain killer on board. That would be helpful.
May I ask some questions before I bring some medicine?
Do you have any allergies to the medicine or Did you take any alcohol?

No, I don't think so.

Okay, I will come back right away for you, sir.

(*In a while*)

Excuse me. sir. Here's your medicine and a glass of warm water.
I hope you feel better after taking a rest.

Thank you so much! I will.

My pleasure. Please let me know if you need any help. I'll be right back.

SITUATION 3 Sick passenger about Indigestion

Excuse me. sir. Are you all right? You look pale a bit.

Oh, thank you for recognizing me. I have really bad indigestion.
I feel uncomfortable because I have indigestion
Do you have anything I can take?

Yes, we do. sir. We have medicine for indigestion on board.
Do you have pain anywhere else?

No, I don't. I think it'll get better if I just take the medicine for indigestion.

Certainly, sir. Just a moment, I will come back shortly.

(*After a while*)

Here you are. You can dissolve the medicine in water and take it.
I hope you get better. sir. If you need anything, please feel free to contact me.

Thank you for your help.

My pleasure sir.

SITUATION 4 Sick passenger about Airsickness

Excuse me, ma'am, Are you alright?

No, I don't think so, I feel dizzy and nauseous.

There is an airsickness bag in your pocket in front of you. You can use that if you need, ma'am. Is there anything I can do for you?

Do you have any medicine for airsickness?

Yes, we do, Are you allergic to any medicine?

No, I'm not.

Just a moment, please. I'll get it for you.

(*In a while*)

Excuse me, ma'am. Here is your medicine with a glass of water.
Please let me know if it's not good even after taking medicine.

Okay, I will.

SITUATION 5 Follow up for sick passenger

(*After 30 minutes, cabin crew have to check passenger whether they are okay*)

How are you feeling now ma'am. Are you still feeling bad?

I feel much better now. Thank you for your consideration.

I'm so happy to hear that. If there is anything I can do for you, just let me know. I will be right back with you.

Take turns practicing role-playing with your partners.

Situation 1. In-flight medical issue - Headache

Situation 2. In-flight medical issue - Catch a cold

Situation 3. In-flight medical issue - Indigestion

Situation 4. In-flight medical issue - Airsickness

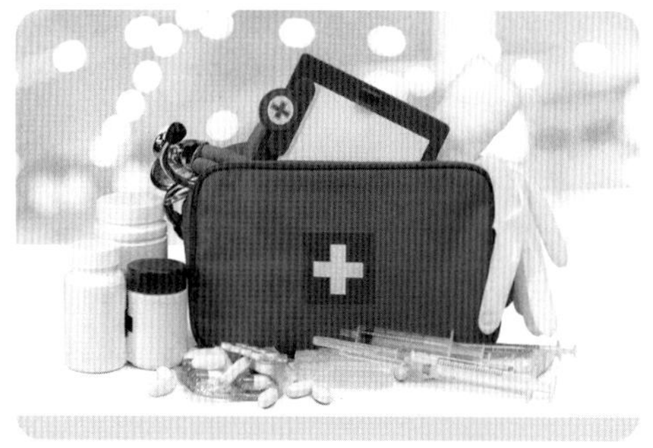

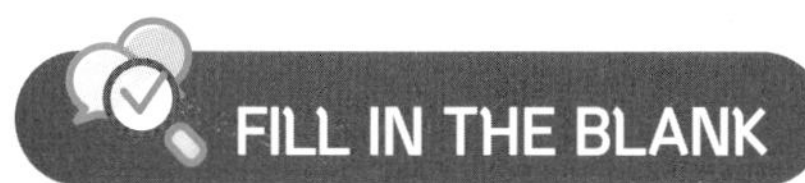

FILL IN THE BLANK

Medicine Symptoms Allergic Free Airsickness

1. May I ask that you have any other ____________?

2. There is an ____________ bag in your pocket in front of you.

3. If you need anything, please feel ____________ to contact me.

MATCH

A. I 'll bring it to you	•	•	1. feeling better
B. I hope you are	•	•	2. hear that
C. I am sorry to	•	•	3. just let me know
D. May I ask some question before	•	•	4. I bring some medi-cine
E. If there is anything I can do for you	•	•	5. right away.

TRANSLATE BETWEEN KOREAN AND ENGLISH

1. 다음 문장을 영어로 바꾸어 보세요.

① 손님, 혹시 약에 대한 알레르기나, 기내에서 알코올음료를 섭취하셨습니까?

____.

② 실례합니다. 여기 약과 따뜻한 물 있습니다.

____.

③ 필요한 게 있으시면 언제든지 문의해주세요.

____.

2. 다음 문장을 한국어로 바꾸어 보세요

① May I ask that you have any other symptoms?

____.

② There is an airsickness bag in your pocket in front of you.

____.

③ I will come back right away for you, sir.

____.

ROLE PLAY

Situation

What would you do if a passenger had a headache on board?

Your Action

____.

INTERVIEW QUESTIONS

Question 1

What is the qualification the cabin crew have in the medical situation on board?

Answer 1

____.

Question 2

What is the qualification the cabin crew have in the medical situation on board?

Answer 2

____.

직무설명

고객 불만 응대 방식 LAST 절차

- Listen(경청)
- Apologize sincerely(사과)
- Showing empathy(공감)
- Task / Aternative solution(대체서비스)

기내에서 발생할 수 있는 컴플레인 종류

- Special Meal (특별식사가 탑재되지 않은 상황)
- Additional Meal Request (추가 식사를 요청하는 상황)
- The Choice of Meal is Out of Stock(요청한 식사가 다 떨어진 상황)
- Drunken Passenger(만취 상태에서 술을 요청하는 상황)
- Spilled Drink on a Passenger(음료를 쏟은 상황)
- Kiz meal offering Situation(어린이 식사 관련 상황)
- Duty-free Item is Sold Out (원하는 면세품이 없는 상황)
- Cabin Temperature (기내 온도로 추위를 호소하는 상황)
- Turbulence (난기류 상황)
- Seating Arrangement (좌석 배정 상황)

Unit 2

Customer complain

고객 불만 사항

Vocabulary

No.	English	Korean
1	Unruly	다루기 힘든, 제멋대로 구는
2	Cooperation	협력, 협조, 협동
3	Lukewarm	미지근한, 미적지근한
4	Heat up	-을 뜨겁게[따뜻하게] 데우다(Warm up)
5	Adjust	조정[조절]하다, 적응하다
6	Appropriate	적절한
7	Blanket	담요
8	Cabin temperature	기내(객실) 온도
9	In-flight entertainment	기내 오락 시스템
10	Reset	다시 맞추다, 고정하다
11	Remote control	리모컨
12	Inconvenience	불편, 애로

I 'll **heat it up** for you.

warm it up

Can I bring you new wine while you are **waiting**.

wait for a while.

wait for minute.

We will check whether the temperature in the cabin is **appropriate** or not

right

proper

suitable

It will take about 15 minutes to heat up **properly**.

fully.

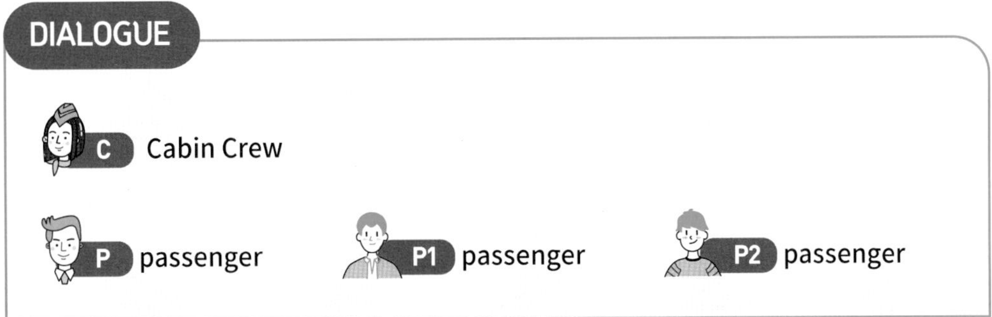

DIALOGUE
C Cabin Crew
P passenger
P1 passenger
P2 passenger

SITUATION 1 Complain about Unruly children

Excuse me. I am trying to get some sleep, but those little boys are making a lot of noise. Could you do something about it?

I am sorry sir, just a moment. Please.
hello, what's your name?

Anny.

what's yours?

Sandy.

Do you like to draw? We have a lovely present for you. it contains pen, color paper and stickers, do you want to have them?

Yes, please.

While I am preparing your gift, I can also prepare your drink and snake.

What would you like to drink? We have orange juice, coke and water.

Can I have orange juice?

Okay, I will come back soon with your drink and gift.

Can you go back to your seat and wait for me?

Okay.

Thank you for your kindly cooperation.

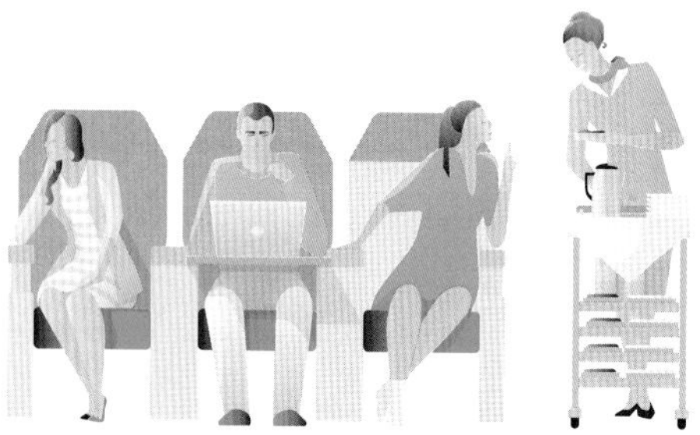

SITUATION 2 Complain about the meal with lukewarm temperature

Excuse me, Can you change this meal to a new one?
this meal is not hot enough and this wine tastes bad.

I am so really sorry sir, I'll heat it up for you.
Can I bring new wine while you are waiting.

(*After a while*)

Excuse me sir. Here is some fresh wine for you

Thank you. What about my meal?

We are heating up your meal now. It will take about 15 minutes to heat up properly.
May I offer one more fresh bread for you? Is that okay?

Okay.

(*A while after*)

Excuse me sir, I am so sorry to keep you waiting.
Here is your meal. I hope it is hot enough.

Thank you.

SITUATION 3 Complain about Cabin temperature

Excuse me, I think the cabin is quite cold now. Can you adjust the temperature?

I am so sorry ma'am. We will check whether the temperature in the cabin is appropriate or not. In the meanwhile, May I offer you an extra blanket or hot beverage for you.
It will warm up your body a little.

Yes, please. Can I have a hot coffee then?

Certainly ma'am. I will come back shortly.

(*After a while*)

Excuse me ma'am. Here is your hot coffee and another blanket.
I reported to our purser that the temperature in the plane is cold.
It will take some time to adjust the temperature.

Thank so much.

Your welcome.

GROUP ACTIVITY

Take turns practicing role-playing with your partners.

Situation 1. Customer's Complain about Unruly children

Situation 2. Customer's Complain about the meal with lunk warm temperature

Situation 3. Customer's Complain about Cabin temperature

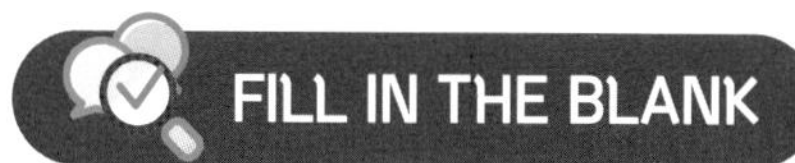

Heat up, Adjust, Additional, Extra, Change

1. It will take about 15 minutes to ________ properly.

2. May I offer you ________ blanket or hot beverage for you.

3. It will take some time to ________ the temperature.

A. I think I need to reset •

B. Can I bring you new wine •

C. We will check whether the temperature in the cabin •

D. My monitor is not working. •

E. Please do not touch the remote control •

• 1. while you are waiting.

• 2. is appropriate or not

• 3. it does not turn on.

• 4. while the system is reset.

• 5. the system in your seat.

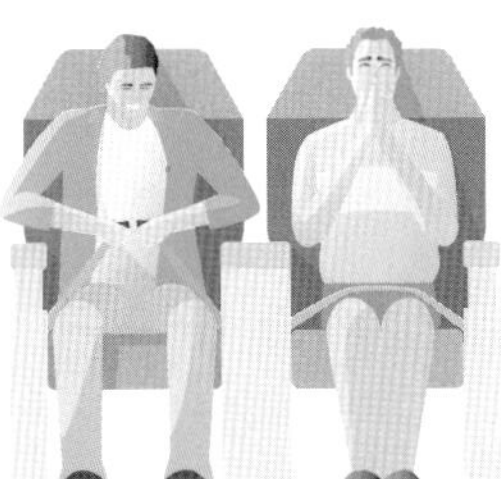

TRANSLATE BETWEEN KOREAN AND ENGLISH

1. 다음 문장을 영어로 바꾸어 보세요.

❶ 바로 음식을 데워드리겠습니다.

______________________________.

❷ 추가 담요와 따뜻한 음료 제공해 드려도 될까요?

______________________________.

❸ 자리의 시스템을 초기화해드리겠습니다.

______________________________.

2. 다음 문장을 한국어로 바꾸어 보세요

❶ Can I bring new wine while you are waiting.

______________________________.

❷ Here is your hot coffee and another blanket.

______________________________.

❸ It will take about 15 minutes to reset your system

______________________________.

Situation

What would you do if a passenger complained about the service?

Your Action

____.

____.

INTERVIEW QUESTIONS

Question 1

How do you handle upset customers?

Answer 1

____.

Question 2

Have you dealt with demanding customers?

Answer 2

____.

직무설명

기내 안전문제 – 난기류(Turbulence)

- 난기류가 발생하면, 기장은 안전 벨트표시등을 켠다.
- 객실 승무원 중 기내 방송이 가능한 승무원은 기내방송을 실시 한다.
- 다른 객실 승무원은 기내로 나가 승객들의 안전 벨트 착용을 지시한다.
- 난기류가 심할경우, 기내 서비스 제공이 제한될수 있다.

기내 안전문제 – 기내 흡연(smoking)

- 기내에서 흡연한 승객이 발각 될 경우, 승객에게 기내에서 흡연은 금지 되어 있음을 상기 시킨다.
- 기내의 흡연 상황을 기장, 사무장, 다른 객실승무원과 기내 흡연 상황을 보고한다.
- 각 항공사의 기내 흡연 상황의 매뉴얼에 따라 신속히 처리 한다.

Unit 3

Safety issue
안전문제

Vocabulary of In-flight Service

No.	English	Korean
1	Turbulence	난기류
2	For your own safety	손님의 안전을 위해서
3	Cigarette	담배
4	Allow	허용하다.
5	Airport police	공항 경찰
6	Against	…에 반대하여[맞서]
7	Disturb	방해하다
8	Report	알리다, 전하다, 보고하다
9	Baby bassinet	아기 요람
10	Lap	무릎
11	Set to	설정하다
12	Flight mode	비행모드

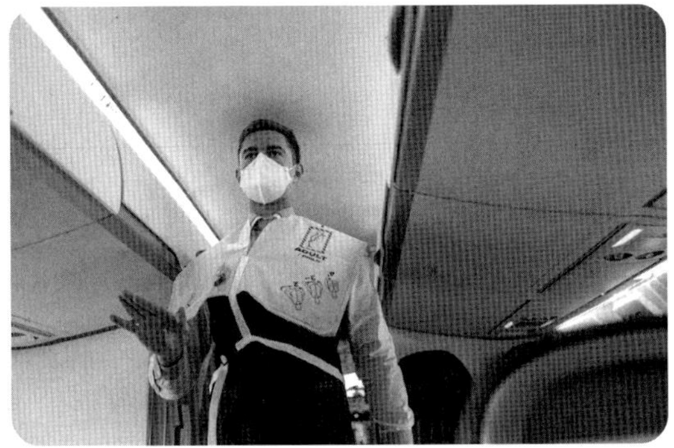

Practical Expression

Thank you for your **cooperation**.
support.
understanding.

This is for **all your safety**.
own your safety.

By the aviation law, smoking is not allowed in any area on board.
According to aviation law,

We are going to **land shortly**.
take off soon.

You have to set it to flight mode **during the flight**.
during the taking off.
during the landing.

DIALOGUE

SITUATION 1 Safety issue for seatbelt sign on

C: Please return to your seat and fasten your seatbelt, ma'am

P: I want to go to the toilet now. I won't be long.

C: I am sorry ma'am. The captain has turned on the fasten seat belt sign.
You are not allowed to use the toilet at this moment for your own safety.

P: That would be a problem for going to the toilet now?

C: Due to turbulence, I am asking you to go back to your seat and fasten the seat belt until the seat belt is off for your own safety.

P: Well, okay I will.

C: Thank you for your cooperation.

SITUATION 2 Safety issue for smoking passenger

Excuse me, sir. Please put out your cigarette and come out of the bathroom now.

What is the problem?

Sir, by the aviation law, smoking is not allowed in any area on board.

I am sorry. I put out my cigarette already. It could be okay.

I have to inform you that smoking is against the law and I have to report to the captain and the airport police. Can I have your passport and seat number please?

Oh, Here you are.

SITUATION 3 Safety issue for passengers who refuse to do safety duty.

Safety check- baby bassinet

Excuse me sir, Can I collect your baby bassinet? We are going to land shortly.

Oh, right now? I don't want to wake my baby because he's sleeping deeply.
Can you come back a little later?

I think you need to hold the baby now, put her on your lap and fasten your seat belt.
This is all for your safety. It is not safe to land with a baby bassinet. Can you do that now?

Oh, okay. Can you help me a little?

Of course, sir. Thank you for your cooperation.

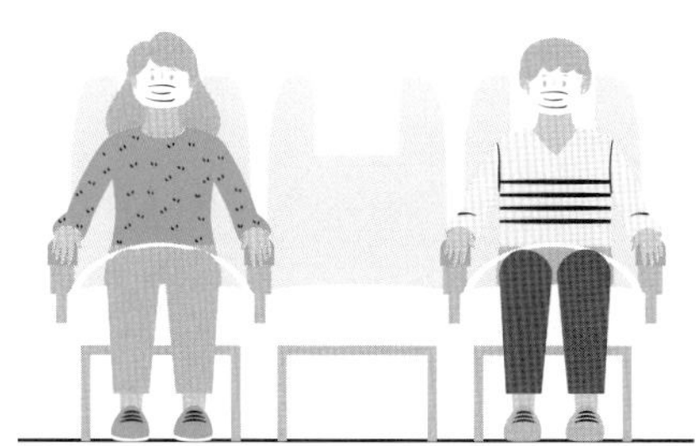

Safety check- electronic devices

Excuse me sir, May I ask that your cell phone is set to flight mode?

I don't think so. Is there a problem with that?

You have to set it to flight mode during the flight.

Oh, I see, I will then.

Thank you for your cooperation.

GROUP ACTIVITY

Take turns practicing role-playing with your partners.

Situation 1. Safety issue with seat belt sign on

Situation 2. Safety issue with smoking passenger

Situation 3. Safety issue with passenger who refuse safety check (baby bassinet)

Situation 4. Safety issue with passenger who refuse safety check (electronic devices)

Fasten, Allowed, As long as, Safety, Flight mode

1. Please return to your seat and ____________ your seatbelt, ma'am

2. You are not ____________ to use the toilet at this moment for your own safety.

3. May I ask that your cell phone is set to __________?

A. You are not allowed to use the toilet at this moment •

B. I inform you that smoking is •

C. It is not safe to land •

D. Could you please set to •

E. Due to turbulence •

• 1. for your own safety.

• 2. against the law

• 3. with baby bassinet.

• 4. flight mode for landing.

• 5. I am asking you to go back to your seat

TRANSLATE BETWEEN KOREAN AND ENGLISH

1. 다음 문장을 영어로 바꾸어 보세요.

① 기장이 안전벨트 사인 등을 켰습니다.

______________________________.

② 기내에서 흡연이 금지되어 있음을 알려드립니다.

______________________________.

③ 아기 요람을 수거해도 될까요?

______________________________.

2. 다음 문장을 한국어로 바꾸어 보세요

① You are not allowed to use the toilet at this moment for your own safety.

______________________________.

② By the aviation law, smoking is not allowed in any area on board.

______________________________.

③ Put her on your lap and fasten your seat belt.

______________________________.

ROLE PLAY

Situation

What would you do if the customer did not cooperate with safety duty on a board?

Your Action

____.

____.

INTERVIEW QUESTIONS

Question 1

Why do you think it is important to keep a regulation?

Answer 1

____.

Question 2

Do you have any experience that you showed initiatives to customers?

Answer 2

____.

참고문헌

- 항공객실서비스영어, 최경희, 윤선정, 한올출판사
- (PDF) English for Cabin Crew | Oxford Express Series | Olivia O. S. - Academia.edu
- English for Cabin Crew(ircambridge.com)
- NCS. 승객탑승 전 준비(박지영)
- NCS. 기내일상안전관리(홍영식)
- Practical English Airline Service, 마근정 외, 한올출판사
- Real English for Cabin Crew 실무편(divii.org)

항공 서비스 영어

저자 소개

| 박미애

세종대학교 관광대학원 관광경영 석사
現) 백석대학교 항공서비스학과 겸임교수
신라대학교 항공서비스학과 겸임교수
에듀윙 대표
前) 서울문화예술대학교 항공서비스학과 외래교수
카타르항공 객실승무원(First & Business Class)
에어부산 1기 객실승무원

| 서희연

現) 경기대학교 관광전문대학원 관광사업경영 석사 과정 中
강동대학교 항공서비스과 겸임교수
오산대학교 항공서비스과 외래강사
SK하이닉스, LG, CJ제일제당, 쿠팡 등 대기업 임직원 비즈니스 영어회화 강사
前) 카타르항공 부사무장
타이거항공 객실승무원

| 황정원

現) ANC 승무원 학원 외항사 강사 다수 외항사 1차 면접관
前) 에미레이트 항공 객실승무원
두바이 kotra 무역 통역
경기도 주최 G-fair 두바이 통역
한국산업인력공단 중동 및 일본어 연수과정 영어인터뷰 전문강사
삼육대학교 취업 멘토링 특강

| 김은혜

세종대학교 관광대학원 항공경영 석사
호주 Sarina Russo hospitality manage ment 전문학사
現) 백석예술대학교 항공서비스 겸임교수
제니쌤의 외항사 과외 대표
외국항공사 객실승무원 1차 면접관(핀에어, 에티오피아항공, 걸프항공 등)
前) 두원공과대학교 항공서비스 외래교수
서울문화예술대학교 항공서비스 외래교수
아세아 항공직업 전문대학교 강사
에어아시아 엑스 항공 객실승무원
에티하드 항공 객실승무원
알리탈리아 항공 통역 승무원

항공 서비스 영어

초판 1쇄 인쇄 2023년 7월 10일
초판 1쇄 발행 2023년 7월 15일

저 자 박미애 · 서희연 · 황정원 · 김은혜
펴낸이 임순재
펴낸곳 (주)한올출판사
등 록 제11-403호
주 소 서울시 마포구 모래내로 83(성산동 한올빌딩 3층)
전 화 (02) 376-4298(대표)
팩 스 (02) 302-8073
홈페이지 www.hanol.co.kr
e-메일 hanol@hanol.co.kr
ISBN **979-11-6647-360-9**

항공 서비스 영어

항공 서비스 영어

항공 서비스 영어

Airline Services English